Original title:
Finding Life's Meaning Between Naps

Copyright © 2025 Creative Arts Management OÜ
All rights reserved.

Author: Jasper Montgomery
ISBN HARDBACK: 978-1-80566-055-2
ISBN PAPERBACK: 978-1-80566-350-8

The Breath of a Slow Afternoon

In a haze of sunlight's glow,
The pillow whispers soft and low.
Socks mismatched, the cat's aloof,
I snooze while chasing dreams aloof.

Time drips like honey on toast,
The couch, my kingdom, I love the most.
With eyelids fluttering like a song,
I wonder where an hour went wrong.

Unraveling Mysteries in Dreams

What is this place of candy clouds?
A parade of llamas saying loud.
I laugh in my slumber, chase rainbows,
As ice cream falls like confetti shows.

Oh, the puzzles that sleep unwinds,
With jellybeans and flying pines.
Logic takes a coffee break,
While I race rabbits in a cake.

Life Unfurling Between Blinks

Between the yawns, the world can glow,
Mice wearing hats, putting on a show.
With a stretch, my mind takes flight,
To places bizarre, oh what a sight!

Each blink, a flip of the script,
Life's circus acts in naps equipped.
When eyelids close, the show begins,
And I'm the star with goofy grins.

Still Waters of the Mind

In stillness, thoughts begin to swirl,
Like strange fish wiggling, giving a twirl.
I ponder if the fridge has flung,
A hidden treasure; what joy it'd bring!

With wisdom brewed in afternoon naps,
I leap on clouds as the world collapses.
Each day a comedy; oh so absurd,
Where snacks are gold and snoring's heard.

Twilight Reflections

In the soft light before the dream,
I ponder the world, it seems so supreme.
My pillow whispers secrets of old,
A tale of the naps where wonders unfold.

A sandwich half-eaten, crumbs in my hair,
Awakening to snickers from thin air.
What did I miss in that brief escapade?
Oh, the circus of thoughts that happily parade.

Serendipity at Siesta

As the sun tilts low, I drift away,
In the hammock's embrace, I wish to stay.
A flurry of dreams, both silly and bright,
Where unicorns drink tea and all feels just right.

With snoring as music, the world slows down,
My cat's gentle purring, the queen of the crown.
A sudden hiccup brings laughter anew,
A comedy show, just me and my shoe.

Sweetness in Stillness

Oh, the sweetness of moments when time stands still,
In the quiet of day, my heart gets its fill.
With drowsy delight, I'm lost in a trance,
As the ceiling transforms to a dance of romance.

A nap is a treasure, it opens the door,
To realms where the nonsense is never a bore.
In pillow fort kingdoms, I reign with a grin,
As the nap time adventures of whimsies begin.

The Echo of the Unconscious

In a land of odd dreams, I gallop on cheese,
With giant marshmallows, a soft, fluffy breeze.
The echo of giggles ricochets through my mind,
As I tumble through naps, delightful and blind.

When slumber's sweet call is a chorus of cheer,
Every wink sheds a layer, my frown disappears.
Awakening puzzled, I giggle with glee,
Who knew naps held secrets so funny and free?

Finding Yourself in Reverie

In a blanket cocoon, I drift away,
Chasing sheep that hop and play.
Dreams of snacks invade my mind,
While the clock ticks—a thief unkind.

Cereal boxes dance in delight,
As I snooze away my waking fight.
Pillow fights with thoughts untamed,
In naps, my quirky fun is claimed.

The Dreamer's Odyssey

On the couch, I embark on a quest,
To uncharted lands where I can rest.
With snores as my battle cry,
In the world of dreams, I learn to fly.

Adventurous cats wear crowns of cheese,
While I conquer realms with expert ease.
Though the snack drawer calls my name,
My dreams of chips are close to fame.

Hints of Hope in Restfulness

Beneath an eyelid, miracles bloom,
In a world where I can zoom.
Giant burgers roll in the breeze,
While penguins slide with such great ease.

Each doze a treasure, each yawn a gift,
In naps, I find my spirits lift.
When laughter dances on the puffy sheets,
I awaken, happy for small treats.

Daylight at the Edge of Slumber

Morning coffee, sweet and hot,
But soon the nap's enticing plot.
I venture forth on a fluffy cloud,
In dreams, I'm bold and oh so proud.

Tickling blankets whisper my name,
Every wink's a little game.
So here I float, on a dreamy ride,
With giggles and snacks by my side.

Quietude's Aha! Moments

In a world that spins so fast,
Sometimes dreams come true at last.
A blanket hug, a cozy seat,
Where scattered thoughts and silence meet.

The cat's curled tight upon my lap,
I drift away, oh sweet mishap!
When dozing off, I start to muse,
About my socks and flavor of booze.

A snack remains, it's gone in dreams,
I wake confused, or so it seems.
Did I just see a flying cat?
Oh wait, that was my old straw hat.

Between the snores, a giggle brews,
Life's big questions stretch like snooze.
What's the meaning? Who can tell?
I blame it all on my dream spell.

Slumber's Silent Epiphanies

In the land of nod, ideas flow,
Like rivers wide, they twist and grow.
A fleeting thought, a silly grin,
Who knew that dreams could hold such sin?

A nap leads me to wondrous things,
Like why my toaster always sings.
An epiphany, quite absurd,
What's in that sandwich? I seem disturbed.

The creaky floorboards start to talk,
As I dream-dance like a flock.
I ponder life's sweet, silly quirks,
Then light a fire to my brain, it lurks.

Awake again with crumbs in hand,
Upon these thoughts, I do expand.
Silly dreams, oh what a show,
Who needs coffee? Just let it flow.

Resting in the Interval

In the pause between the crazy,
A sleepy smile makes life hazy.
Dreams of chocolate fill the air,
Is that really why I'm unaware?

The world can wait, I'll take a break,
With midday snoozes, I can shake.
What if gravity starts to lag,
And all my worries fit in a bag?

In slumber, logic takes a snooze,
Where socks dance and the cat can choose.
Each nap a portal to delight,
To figure out if socks are right.

Waking up with drool in tow,
Absurd adventures start to flow.
But what's a nap, if not a quest,
To ponder life while we all rest?

Soulful Pause

Oh, the joy of afternoon,
A gentle hum, a sleepy tune.
Dreams are like balloons, they drift,
Each puffy thought, a cosmic gift.

In that pause, I catch a grin,
Like silly jokes that pull me in.
What's for dinner? Don't have a clue,
In dreamland, I'm the chef, it's true!

I twirl with thoughts beneath the glaze,
Chasing shadows in a playful daze.
Laughter simmers just inside,
As silly notions start to glide.

With sleepy eyes, the world expands,
Who knew the grain of time can dance?
So take a breath and then let go,
Life's big lessons start as a show.

Sleep's Gentle Intermission

In the realm of cozy dreams,
I drift on fluffy seams.
Snores become my funny tune,
While time begins to swoon.

Teddy bears hold secrets tight,
Whispering in the night.
A snack's a hero on this quest,
As naps turn into jest.

Beneath the sun's soft glare,
An armchair is my lair.
With visions of a couch parade,
Who knew sleep was a trade?

With each snooze, a laugh does bloom,
As daydreams fill the room.
Life's meaning hides in every yawn,
As giggles greet the dawn.

The Dance of Daydreams

In a world where pillows sway,
Napping leads the way.
Dancing on the edge of sleep,
Sweet giggles I will keep.

Each dream a silly twist,
On adventures I can't resist.
A goat wearing fancy shoes,
Makes me chuckle with some snooze.

Coffee beans begin to whirl,
As thoughts twirl like a girl.
A cat with a monocle eyes,
Snoozing 'neath the sunny skies.

In this dance, I find my way,
Bouncing lightly in the play.
With every snooze, joy does gleam,
In this whimsical daydream.

Respite and Revelation

Between blinks and buttered toast,
I ponder what I love the most.
Scribbles swirl in my hazy head,
What's more life than a well-placed bed?

Dreams are keys to laughter's gate,
Where goofy thoughts can oscillate.
A dragon rides a bicycle,
Every snooze, a miracle!

Naps are like a late-night snack,
Time for my brain to slouch and slack.
With giggles in each nodding pause,
I strut to my own applause.

Each break is a step on this stage,
As sleep and dreams engage.
With each snooze, I gain a spark,
In this hilarious arc.

Between the Pillows of Thought

Nestled where the soft winds blow,
Is a land where dreamers flow.
With each nap, I catch a grin,
As visions tangled up begin.

Mice in tuxedos play croquet,
While I snuggle my cares away.
The clock ticks in a silly way,
As I snooze the afternoon sway.

To ponder 'midst the cuddly fluff,
Is to know I've had enough.
Each snooze brings clarity so fine,
Wrapped in blankets, my thoughts entwine.

Between each doze, life's a whim,
In the land of napping's hymn.
The meaning winks, mischief in tow,
Laughter's on the pillow's glow.

Awakening in Between Dreams

In snoozeville I reign, all comfy and warm,
With pillows like clouds, where worries transform.
The tick-tock of time, a distant old tune,
I'll conquer the world, but first, another swoon.

With eyelids like curtains, my show's about to start,
Plot twist! I just snored and fell back in the cart.
My dreams throw a party, oh what a delight,
But reality pulls me, 'Hey, get up! It's bright!'

Coffee is calling, a siren so sweet,
Yet snores still echo, a faithful repeat.
Every catnap I take is a journey, you see,
In lands where I'm king, on a soft, fluffy sea.

When finally roused by a child's playful shout,
I ponder if choosing naps is what life's all about.
But the answer can wait, while I blink and I grin,
There's a couch with my name, let the dozing begin.

The Reverie After Slumber

I drift on a cloud, the softest of beds,
Where dreams are the pillows that cradle my heads.
Each yawn a reminder of adventures untold,
In lands where I'm brave—or just slightly bold.

Oh, naps are a treasure, a comedic delight,
Where I rule with aplomb and don't have to fight.
The snacks are delicious, the sun's shining bright,
But alas, there's that clock, oh what a dreadful sight!

Back in the reality where chores loom like ghosts,
I stretch and I sigh at my nap-loving host.
"Just five more," I plead, in a half-closed eye plea,
But nap-time negotiation is tough on me.

Yet here's to the times when dreams meet the day,
With laughter and giggles, like children at play.
In the corridors of naps, life's sweetness I'll glean,
For humor hangs thick in the slumber's unseen.

Whispers of Wakefulness

A nod here, a shift there, a shallow breath sighs,
With whispers of wakefulness and cake in my eyes.
The world pauses slightly, a flicker of peace,
As I conquer my thoughts with naptime's release.

Oh dreams, little jesters, with antics so grand,
Where I'm surfing on rainbows or slipped on quicksand.
A sleepy delight in the oddest of forms,
As I roll on my side, defying all norms.

The clock is a villain with numbers that grew,
While I gather up strength for a nap encore too.
Yet deep in my thoughts, I giggle and grin,
At the funny absurdity where dreams have been.

So raise a glass high to the moments we share,
In the quiet of slumber, stripped down to our care.
With laughter and joy, I'm embracing the dream,
As I snooze through the chaos, or so it would seem.

Moments that Suspend Time

In the realm of the drowsy, time stops in a blink,
When eyelids grow heavy and dreams start to sink.
A catnap is joy, a cheeky little scheme,
Where all of my worries dissolve in a dream.

With pillows as ships, we sail on soft seas,
As I navigate laughter on gentle, wild breeze.
Each snore is a wave, a chuckle, a burst,
And here comes the reason that naps might be cursed.

Awake, I find crumbs of joy on my shirt,
From a midnight snack, the evidence flirt.
I giggle at life's sweet and silly charade,
As I find hidden treasures in snooze time parade.

With a wink to the day and a laugh at fate's game,
I ponder on nonsense that's never the same.
So here's to those moments, a pause in the grind,
In the laughter of naps, life's magic I'll find.

Tranquility's Unexpected Wisdom

In a world that spins with haste,
I seek my pillow's warm embrace.
A nap's a treasure, oh so grand,
Where wisdom drifts like grains of sand.

The cat sprawls wide; I take my cue,
To snooze away the day, it's true!
In dreams, I'm grand, a boss supreme,
While napping lends a blissful gleam.

With every yawn, the world grows dim,
I close my eyes, start to swim.
In slumber's arms, I find my cheer,
Awake to laughter, that's sincere!

So here's to naps, my faithful friends,
Where thought is free and time transcends.
In playful dreams, I find the light,
Until it's time to wake, take flight!

Light Falls Between the Breaths

As clock hands tick, I drift away,
In dreams, I dance and sway.
The nap, a spark of silly delight,
Brings whispers of wisdom in the night.

My sofa hugs, so soft and dear,
Offers solace, draws me near.
With every snooze, I learn the art,
Of laughter hiding in the heart.

I chuckle as I snore with glee,
Conversations with my mug of tea.
Each gentle snort brings forth a grin,
While fleeting thoughts swirl and spin.

In every pause, a story thrives,
While sleepy dreams, they come alive.
Between the breaths, the joy expands,
In cozy realms, I make my plans!

Dreams that Linger

In the afternoon, the world's asleep,
I tiptoe in with dreams to keep.
A nap unravels silly schemes,
As giggles echo through my dreams.

The blanket wraps me like a hug,
Life's a circus, I'm the bug!
With each snore, I take flight high,
On cotton clouds, I laugh and sigh.

Kittens join with frolicking grace,
While opposed to napping is the race.
In slumber's realm, my worries cease,
A nap transforms the world to peace.

So if you seek a jest or two,
Take a chance, slip into the blue.
In dreams that linger, let's unite,
And conspire in the sleep of night!

The Poetry of Pause

Between the whirs and bustling cars,
I craft my world of soft regard.
The magic lies in every pause,
Where nap-turned-wisdom earns applause.

As eyelids droop and laughter flows,
In dreamland, anything goes!
Chasing rainbows, sipping tea,
Playful fables come to me.

I wander realms where socks unite,
And every snooze feels just right.
In whimsical dreams, I feel so free,
As nap time blooms, unexpectedly.

In playful chair and blanketed lane,
Life's lightness dances, free of strain.
So join the fun, embrace the trend,
For joy is wrapped in nap-time's blend!

Restful Echoes

On the couch, I take my seat,
Whispers of dreams, oh so sweet.
Pillow's embrace, a cozy spell,
Reality fades, who can tell?

Naps that stretch like lazy cats,
Mind wanders where the giggle's at.
In slumber's dance, the world feels light,
Counting sheep till they take flight.

Each snooze is like a treasure hunt,
Searching for laughs, oh what a stunt!
Waking just in time for pie,
Life's best moments floating by.

So here's to naps, those quirky trips,
Exploring dreams and tasty quips.
With every doze, a new delight,
In restful echoes, hearts take flight.

The Pause Before the Dawn

When daylight calls, I hit the snooze,
In that moment, I just choose.
Cuddled tight with dreams so bright,
Who needs a day when this feels right?

The sun might rise, but I still lay,
In breezy thoughts, I laugh and play.
Coffee can wait, let me pretend,
That napping is a means to mend.

Counting all the chips and dip,
In dreamland's grasp, I take a trip.
The pause before the world awakes,
Brings silly joy in tiny flakes.

So when the morning taps my door,
I'll stifle yawns and seek out more.
In every nap, a giggle stays,
A secret blessing in sleepy haze.

In Pursuit of Fleeting Thoughts

Chasing dreams like butterflies,
Laughter echoes, while the world sighs.
In a nap, I'll catch a glimpse,
Of half-formed thoughts and silly hints.

Napping's art, a funny game,
Each wink, a spark, I'll never tame.
While others rush, I take my time,
In slumber's grip, it feels sublime.

Thoughts slip by like soap on skin,
Elusive joys are what I win.
A yawning chase for moments pure,
In briefest naps, I feel secure.

When I awake, they slip away,
But laughter lingers, bright as day.
In playful dreams, I often find,
The wittiest of joys unwind.

Daydreams and Gentle Whispers

A soft sigh curls in the air,
Daydreams dance without a care.
With each doze, I drift and sway,
Laughing softly, come what may.

Tick-tocks play in sleepy rounds,
While fantasy upon me bounds.
Gentle whispers weave their tale,
In napping's grace, I will not fail.

What could be with eyelids low,
Adventures start where giggles flow.
Between the snores, the laughter peeks,
In tender dreams, my spirit speaks.

So close your eyes and join the fun,
In whispering dreams, the race is won.
For in the nap, the world takes pause,
In whispers soft, we find our cause.

Sleepy Corners of Contemplation

In the nook where pillows reign,
Thoughts drift soft like cotton wane,
Whispers faint amidst the snores,
Philosophies behind closed doors.

Why ponder life with caffeine rush?
When slumber's there, we need not rush.
The world spins slow in this warm haze,
As dreaming takes us through a maze.

Lattes cool while we droop down,
Wrapping us in comfort's gown.
The answers dance just out of reach,
In four-bedrooms' quite a speech.

Awake, confetti thoughts take flight,
In snoozing, wisdom feels so right.
Naps, the tutors of our lore,
Unwrap the truth behind the snore.

The Heart's Gentle Sigh

A yawn escapes, the world's on pause,
With dreams of cake and sunshine's cause.
In every doze, a giggle hides,
As everyday nonsense coincides.

Beneath the blanket's cozy shell,
Life's riddle wraps us like a spell.
Chuckles float on snoozes deep,
In fluffy clouds, we seam our sleep.

The heart beats soft beneath the sheets,
Dreams tap-dance on our fuzzy feats.
With laughter echoing in the night,
Even worries seem just light.

Awake, we grin at life's crescendo,
Choosing joy amidst a nap's mellow.
In tender sighs, we truly find,
The punchline of a clever mind.

Harvesting Dreams

In a field of fluffy white,
Where daylight yields to cozy night,
We plant our thoughts like crops of cheer,
And reap the giggles year after year.

Napping's art, a joyous flair,
Painting dreams with dozy care.
We gather thoughts like golden grain,
In the tractor's hum, there's no disdain.

Cows chew cud while we ponder pause,
Tickling thoughts without a cause.
The world outside can whirl and dance,
But here, we take our blissful chance.

With snores as tunes, we harvest light,
Our dreams take flight, a silly sight.
In laughter's field, so oh-so grand,
We find delight in dreamland's hand.

The Sweet Embrace of Stillness

In the quiet of the midday glow,
Sleep whispers secrets soft and slow.
We lounge in corners, slack and spry,
While ponderings twirl, oh my, oh my!

A comfy chair, a sunbeam's kiss,
In stillness, we find such bliss.
With chuckles brewing like tea on the stove,
Life's puzzle pieces settle and rove.

As clocks tick-tock, we chuckle low,
In drowsy ponderings, wisdom will grow.
With every blink, a laugh may spring,
'Cause life's a jolly, quirky fling!

In the arms of calm, we dance awhile,
Finding joy in every sleepy mile.
So let the world just whir and whirl,
For naps bring laughter to this twirl.

Introspection in the In-Between

In the quiet moments, eyes shut tight,
Thoughts drift and wander, taking flight.
Dreams tease the edges of sleepy embrace,
While my blanket becomes a familiar space.

Pillow whispers secrets, soft and sweet,
Each snooze a riddle, a tasty treat.
Should I ponder deep truths or just doze?
A dilemma that only the dozer knows.

Cereal bowls clank, a breakfast delay,
While the universe unfolds in my inner ballet.
Are these visions profound or just plain bizarre?
Maybe it's genius, or a nap too far!

Suddenly I wake, with crumbs on my chin,
Philosophy or snack? Which one did I win?
With pillows as mentors, my mind takes a leap,
In the gaps between snoozes, wisdom runs deep.

Cradled by Calm

Nestled in comfort, I close my eyes,
Where dreams float like clouds in wide open skies.
Each yawn a reminder of life's gentle tease,
As I navigate worlds on a soft, cozy breeze.

Blankets cocoon me in warmth and delight,
Snuggles and laughter pillow-fight the night.
Do I drift to a sea of profound revelation,
Or chase after thoughts with no end destination?

Time seems elastic in this lull of repose,
As hiccups of wisdom erupt like a rose.
Should I ponder my purpose or just snooze some more?
The answer's elusive, like socks on the floor!

With dreams in my pocket, I float back to play,
Worlds made of jellybeans leading the way.
In this bliss of the in-between, I cheerfully laugh,
For life's little meanings are found in the half.

A Dance of Consciousness and Dreams

Bouncing between slumber and the bright light of day,
Each nap an adventure, a brief getaway.
I twirl in my blanket, a waltz with the air,
Chasing after thoughts that float everywhere.

Time slips away like a glimmering fish,
The moment I ponder, I wake with a swish.
Why is the couch both my throne and my bed?
In this kingdom of cushions, I rule my own head.

Sleep is a party where dreams do the jig,
Every snooze a encore, let's dance with a wig!
What's real or a figment, who really can tell?
Maybe a pillow is an oracle's shell!

So here in the chaos of naps and of dreams,
Life wraps around me in whimsical seams.
With giggles and snickers, I seize the day's fun,
In this sleepy ballet, I've already won!

Echoes of Daylight Dreams

In twilight's embrace, we glide,
Chasing shadows far and wide.
Pillow whispers, secrets told,
Adventures in slumber, bold.

Jellybean clouds drift on by,
Lemonade streams of a pie in the sky.
Clock hands dance a lazy beat,
As snores compose our rhythmic feat.

Scattered thoughts like confetti rain,
In this realm, there's no such pain.
Floating on a hammock's swing,
Awake or asleep, we're still the king.

So, grab your dreams and take a nap,
In this funny, cozy trap.
Laughter echoes through the air,
Life's grand circus, we're all the flair.

The Rapture of Rest

In the land of nod, we feast,
A sugar rush without a beast.
Zany roles we play all night,
Sleeping lands filled with delight.

Socks turned puppets, blankets flow,
Napping stars put on a show.
Doughnut dreams and soda streams,
Reality slips, bursting seams.

We tango with the sheep at play,
Counting nonsense dreams away.
Silly hats and ice cream cones,
Life's a giggle between our moans.

So let the snooze take center stage,
In this humorous, sleepy page.
Awake or dim, we celebrate,
In nap's sweet rapture, it's never late.

Slices of Thought During Naps

Cucumber slices on my eyes,
Sunshine pizza in the skies.
Thoughts sprout like daisies' bloom,
In my cozy, sleepy room.

Silly ideas race in a blur,
What to wear? A giant fur!
Riding bears or jumping jacks,
Life's a hoot from cozy snacks.

Between soft pillows, schemes take flight,
A world of nonsense, pure delight.
Lollypops raining from above,
Every nap filled with doodles of love.

So, as I drift on clouds of fluff,
Know that napping's more than enough.
In these slices, laughs and dreams,
Reality's lost in giggly streams.

Sunlit Moments of Closure

Daylight fades with a sleepy grin,
Waking dreams, where fun begins.
Sunlit moments softly play,
In a cozy, napping way.

Feathered pillows whisper low,
Curious critters put on a show.
Juggling ducks and swirling pies,
Endless laughter as time flies.

Chewy caramel twists of thought,
A treasure map that naps have brought.
Silly riddles bounce around,
In the bliss of dreams unbound.

So here's to naps, our secret muse,
In playful slumber, we can't lose.
Sunlit laughter, a sweet delight,
Where dreams and giggles shine so bright.

Echoes of a Hibernating Heart

In fluffy realms where dreams take flight,
   Beneath a blanket, snug and tight.
   The world outside fades to a hum,
While I drift off to the sound of fun.

   The coffee brews but I just snore,
   As life dances by, what a chore!
     Bears have got it figured out,
   In their caves, they lounge about.

A snack or two might grace my day,
But first, a snooze—who needs to play?
The fridge can wait, oh dear sweet fate,
   At leisure's door, I contemplate.

In dreams, the snacks are endless treats,
  Life's great answers reside in sheets.
   So here I lay, untangling time,
   In naps, I find a rhythm sublime.

Crumbs of Wisdom in a Sleepy State

A yawn escapes, the day feels wrong,
Yet wisdom's whispers hum along.
Pillow talk with pillows bold,
Reveals deep truths, or so I'm told.

Sleepy chatter from my worn-out self,
Dreams are close, just an old book's shelf.
Naps reveal what life's about,
Between the snores, I laugh and shout.

Shall I rise? Oh, what a jest!
The couch declares it's for the best.
Mind adrift, concerns deflate,
Napping's really first-rate fate.

Yet crumbs of thought fall here and there,
As I feast upon my fuzzy chair.
A sleepy sage in soft repose,
Who needs to think when dreaming glows?

Dialogue with the Dawn

The sun peeks in with a cheeky grin,
Whispering truths where naps begin.
"Awake, oh sleepyhead!" it sings,
But dreams have truths, oh precious things.

I stretch and roll, but nap's allure,
Calls me back with its cozy cure.
"Why rush to catch life's buzzing scene?
The best advice is in soft sheen."

With twinkling stars still in the sky,
"Sleep more!" I yell, and oh how I sigh.
Morning coffee? Let's delay,
It's more fun in dreams, I say!

Chasing thoughts in a slumber dance,
Who needs plans when you can prance?
Each nap is filled with witty jest,
In the realm of rest, I'm truly blessed.

Embracing the Drift

In the lazy lap of afternoon,
I find my comfy sleep cocoon.
Time slips by with a giggling sway,
As I float in dreams, oh what a play!

The clock's tick-tock feels like a song,
"Stay here!" it croons, "You can't go wrong!"
Images swirl, and laughter erupts,
Napping heroes, we're blissfully corrupted.

The world outside flits in a race,
While I glide through a dreamy space.
Tickled by thoughts both funny and grand,
I snooze away with a soft, warm hand.

Embracing the drift is an art so fine,
The secrets of life in each sleepy line.
So join me here, where the breezes twine,
Between the naps, the stars align.

Ripples of Insight

In the midst of z's we float,
Dreams drift in a cozy boat.
Each snore a wave of deep thought,
New wisdom found in a snooze caught.

Laughter echoes in the mist,
With every nap, a clever twist.
Pillow fights with pillow knights,
Conversations lost in sleepy heights.

A sandwich shared with a teddy,
Thoughts are lazy but oh so heady.
The clock spins on a comical spin,
Awakening brings reflections in.

Sunlight winks through lazy blinds,
Funny moments in the binds.
Resting in bliss, we reunite,
Each nap a spark, a burst of light.

Murmurs in the Afterglow

After dreams, the whispers play,
Tickling thoughts that drift away.
Silly faces, hidden smiles,
Resting heroes across the miles.

With a yawn, the day begins,
Socks mismatched, haphazard wins.
Murmurs mix with sleepy sighs,
In the glow, the laughter flies.

Twirling thoughts on little wings,
Napping kings and laughter brings.
A jester's crown upon our heads,
Serious quests from sleepy beds.

As we stretch, the world takes shape,
Awake, we plot the day's escape.
Crafting joy in a slumber's spell,
Murmurs linger, all is well.

In the Cradle of Quiet

Nestled in the softest space,
A tickled thought, a funny face.
In this cradle where dreams abide,
Curiosity starts to ride.

Whispers of snacks and silly pranks,
Naps are treasure, oh, the thanks!
A wink from shadows where we lie,
Good humor dances, oh so sly.

Chasing clouds with napping dreams,
Sipping sunshine, bursting seams.
In quiet moments, giggles burst,
The joy of napping is the first.

Rest assured, the world can wait,
In slumber, we discover fate.
Each snooze is quite the clever plot,
In the cradle, we lose the knot.

Embracing the Interlude

Between the ticks of time we play,
Napping moments on the way.
With a stretch, we take a seat,
Life's ambrosia, oh so sweet.

Caterpillars dream of flight,
In cozy dreams, they get it right.
Whimsical thoughts like popcorn pop,
In this interlude, the laughter drops.

Sandman's dance and blanket fort,
Within is laughter of the sort.
Cuddled close, we hear the snore,
Life's zany charms we can't ignore.

As the clock hands spin around,
In this space, true joy is found.
Embracing naps, our hearts take flight,
In the interlude, all feels right.

Glimpses Through Squinted Eyes

In sunlight's glow, I doze away,
Dreams dance lightly, then decay.
A snack in hand, ambitions low,
The couch my throne, where rivers flow.

A bird outside sings a sweet tune,
As I drift near a sleepy swoon.
My thoughts get lost in cotton clouds,
Embracing silence, soft and loud.

The cat sprawls wide, a royal way,
In this kingdom of dreams, I stay.
With an egg on toast as my reward,
I wonder here, do naps afford?

When life is busy, I'll press pause,
For meaningful thoughts amidst the snores.
Waking to laughter, I must confess,
Naps are moments I adore best!

Nature's Timeless Intermission

Under trees, the sunbeam plays,
Snoozing mildly through hot days.
A lazy bug on grass does crawl,
While I lie back, a sleepy ball.

Clouds drift by, as I contend,
How do such moments never end?
Dreams take flight on butterfly wings,
A symphony of snores, it sings.

The breeze whispers, 'Just hold tight,'
As eyelids fight with all their might.
In the arms of nature, I find peace,
In this lullaby, my worries cease.

Awake I rise, with crumbs in hand,
Feeling like a dreamy brand.
Each nap a jewel softly gleamed,
In the heart of life, I've dreamt and dreamed.

Whispers of the Half-Asleep

A scratchy blanket, cozy nest,
In pillow clouds, I find my rest.
Dreams wiggle close, like ants in line,
Should I nap more, or just decline?

Outside the world spins on so fast,
While I embrace this snooze spell cast.
A snore escapes, oh dear, how loud!
While wonders whisk me in a shroud.

Fluttering eyelids, cast a spell,
As thoughts of snacks begin to dwell.
A sandwich waits just out of sight,
Too bad I'm lost in dreams of flight.

Soon I'll rise, fresh thoughts in tow,
Adventure calls, though moving slow.
Grinning wide at slumber's bliss,
In every slumber, there's magic in this!

The Slumbering Quest

With a trusty pillow as my guide,
I venture forth, but lay aside.
The quest begins with a single yawn,
As snoozes lead me, dusk till dawn.

Missions from the fridge call my name,
A snack-filled journey, never the same.
Half-asleep, I ponder grand schemes,
While visiting the castle of dreams.

On this grand adventure, I find a chair,
To plot my next snack, with utmost care.
Eyebrows raised, a secret I keep,
Magic happens in dreams so deep.

When I awake, the world seems bright,
With a sense of humor, pure delight.
Each snooze a chapter, each stretch a quest,
In the realm of naps, I'm always blessed!

Floating in the Fog of Dreams

In a world where pillows call,
I drift and float, my thoughts enthrall.
Clouds of snores and giggles gleam,
Life's a puzzle, or so it seems.

A sandwich waits upon my plate,
But dropped it did, oh what a fate!
Between the snoozes, ideas swell,
Like bubbles in a wishing well.

The clock ticks loud, yet I ignore,
As snoozing kitty takes the floor.
Whispers of wisdom, fluffy and light,
Bounce around in dream's delight.

Upon this fluff, I find my way,
In naps, I laugh and dream, and play.
With every yawn, I take my leap,
Where wisdom hides beneath my sleep.

Moments in the Hazy Twilight

In twilight's haze, I stretch and yawn,
The couch is calling, and I'm drawn.
A cosmic quest to find my snack,
Yet here I lie, with limbs go slack.

The comedy of crumbs and cheese,
Faced with hunger while I tease.
My dreams are silly, twisted, and fun,
Bowling with bears, oh what a run!

As sunlight fades, my eyelids soar,
A slumber party with no encore.
Between the giggles, time flies by,
Wrapped in warmth, oh me, oh my!

Each snooze's a tick of life's own beat,
While silly visions dance on repeat.
In naps, I find my jester's lute,
Strumming laughter, oh how cute!

Reflections in a Cozy Slumber

In cozy corners, dreams parade,
With every snore, my worries fade.
Mirrors filled with fluffy fluff,
Speak in riddles, so sweet and tough.

A dance with ducks upon the floor,
Or marching ants out through the door.
In sleepy realms where giggles reign,
It's absurd, and I'm insane!

A blanket fort, my castle grand,
In dreamland, I'm the ruler's hand.
Each nap a quest to find the jest,
In sleepy smiles, I find the best.

As daylight dims, I start to soar,
With dreams that leave me wanting more.
In cozy slumber, laughter spry,
I snooze to thrive, oh my, oh my!

Beneath the Blanket of Life

Beneath the covers, I close my eyes,
As thoughts parade in sleepy skies.
The world spins round, without a care,
A silly dance in misty air.

A nap suggests the fun begins,
Where logic falters, madness wins.
I chase the shadows of twinkling stars,
And find my laughter behind the bars.

The universe, a quilt of joy,
With patches stitched from every toy.
In dreams, I twirl with socks and socks,
Mother's laughter, tick-tock clocks.

Upon this bed of fluff and cheer,
I toss and turn, but hold all dear.
Life's a riddle mixed with glee,
Wrapped in naps, just wait and see!

The Art of Being Half Awake

In dreams, I dance on cotton clouds,
While reality shouts, 'Get up, you loud!'
My pillow's a port in a sleepy storm,
Where lazy thoughts take a snooze form.

The coffee brews like a sleepy brew,
Yet my eyelids weigh a ton, it's true.
With each doze, I plot my grand escape,
A nap is a map—I'll just take the tape.

Conversations fade like distant stars,
While I snuggle up tight with soft cotton bars.
The world spins on like a merry-go-round,
But I'm half-lost in the sleep that I found.

So here's to the art of dozing down,
The masterful craft of the couch-bound crown.
In slumber's embrace, we chase the bizarre,
And wake up laughing—what on earth was that spar?

Cherishing Fleeting Whispers

In sleepy sighs, the secrets weave,
Under quilted dreams where we believe.
A gurgling nap is a fleeting muse,
Stirring thoughts in a half-lit snooze.

The clock ticks softly, a lullaby sweet,
As I embrace cozy, warm retreat.
What wisdom lurks in sleepy delight?
A riddle awaits in the sting of the night.

Between nods and grins, time takes a pause,
Whispering truths without any cause.
The nap gods chuckle from realms I can't see,
While I cradle my doubts and cater to glee.

Fleeting moments of clarity shine,
While my head flops sideways—and oh, that's just fine!
As I muffle a yawn, life saunters on through,
Chasing whimsical thoughts like a deranged zoo.

Ephemeral Clarity

Sleepy sparks, like fireflies bright,
Flicker away when the day turns to night.
In gentle slumber, I ponder and muse,
Is the universe laughing at me while I snooze?

The world's perplexities blur in a haze,
As I float between naps in this sleepy daze.
With blanket as shield, I explore my dreams,
Where nonsense is king, or so it seems.

Awakening slowly, half-sure of the tale,
My thoughts get jumbled, like a ship's tattered sail.
Each nap unravels another wild thread,
As giggles emerge when my brain's half-dead.

Epiphanies flash in a wink or a blink,
While I mutter sagas that perhaps make you think.
But when it's all done, and I'm back in the fray,
I just grab my pillow and doze the day away.

Shadows of the Late Afternoon

Sunlight spills on the floor like a quilt,
Daring me to rise from the couch where I'm built.
But sleepy shadows loom long and wide,
As I wiggle and nestle, my nap-chasing guide.

The world waits outside with its bustling noise,
But here in my cocoon, I've got my joys.
In this dim-lit realm, I'm a king on a throne,
Where the laughter of dreams is my only tone.

Time drips slowly like honey so sweet,
While I drift on waves of a dim afternoon heat.
With pillows as boats, I float on the tide,
Navigating half-thoughts where whimsy can hide.

As the shadows whisper their playful delight,
I chase silly musings till I end my night.
Awake or asleep, what difference does it make?
Every nap taken is a reason to wake.

The Poetry of Dozing

In the chair, I find my muse,
With droopy eyes, I cannot lose.
Thoughts like clouds float by so slow,
Dreams ignite like fireflies' glow.

Pillows soft, they call my name,
Every nap, a brand new game.
Counting sheep in lazy bliss,
Missed my chance for that first kiss!

Snuggled tight in cozy gear,
Life's big questions disappear.
What's the point of nine to five?
I'd rather nap than just survive!

So when the world grows loud and bright,
I close my eyes to chase the light.
In dreams, I laugh and wiggle free,
Napping's my philosophy!

Nirvana in the Nap

Close my eyes to find the bliss,
In the moments I can't miss.
Snoozing deep, I float away,
Waking's just a game I play.

Under blankets, dreams take flight,
Snoring softly, what a sight!
Hungry snacks drift by my side,
In this dreamland, I can glide.

Time drips slowly, like thick cream,
Everything's a silly dream.
Why wake up to daily grinds,
When naps are where true joy unwinds?

So let's toast the midday snooze,
To cozy times, we cannot lose.
Life's big secrets lie in rest,
Nap enthusiasts are the best!

Snoozing Beneath the Stars

Under stars, I stake my claim,
In the night, I play a game.
Moonlight winks, a cheeky tease,
Napping's how I find my ease.

Tickle of the gentle breeze,
Whispers lull me, not a tease.
Dreams with jellybeans take flight,
As I drift into the night.

Counting constellations near,
Each one seems to share a cheer.
Nighttime's magic keeps me close,
In sleep's embrace, I'm not morose!

Lost in dreams of silly quests,
I'm a hero; I'm the best.
With a yawn, I greet the dawn,
Snoozing's where my heart is drawn!

The Lullaby of Purpose

Hum of the day fades like a song,
In my dreams, nothing feels wrong.
Cuddled up in quilted cheer,
Snoozing time is finally here!

Chasing thoughts like frolicking cats,
I sit back, and that's where it's at.
A chuckle bubbles, what a sight,
I'll debate the world—tomorrow night!

Naps are where I find my plan,
With a pillow, I shake a hand.
Life's a giggle, I firmly believe,
In another snooze, I'll soon achieve!

So join me in this cozy play,
We'll nap our worries all away.
With laughter ringing in the air,
Purpose blooms in dreamland's care!

Small Truths of the Snooze

When pillows call like siren songs,
I ponder if I slept too long.
The clock's hands laugh, they tick and tock,
While I dream deep in my cozy rock.

A snack in dreams is quite the treat,
With gummy bears and candy neat.
Yet morning light peeks through the shade,
And back to life, I'm slowly made.

As sirens wail, I resume my quest,
To snooze just one more minute, rest!
The joys of slumber, oh so brief,
Are sweet as cake, yet bring me grief.

Thus nap by nap, I learn it true,
The world can wait, I need my snooze!
A truce with clocks, I boldly strike,
In fluffy joy, I find my hike.

Whims of the Weighted Blanket

A blanket heavy, snuggly, round,
In its embrace, I'm tightly bound.
The weight feels like a hug, I swear,
As I drift off without a care.

Dreams dance around me, joyfully bright,
While I'm encapsulated, snug and tight.
My mind explores a world so grand,
Where jellybeans rain from high up land.

Yet, alas, the clock buzzes loud,
And drags me back to the waking crowd.
But oh! The conflict, a soft delight,
To nap or snack? A daily fight.

The blanket quivers with each sweet sigh,
Whispering secrets of a sleepy pie.
One more dream, one last embrace,
Before I shuffle back to the race.

The Intermission of a Dreamer

In the theater of night, I take my seat,
The credits roll to a dreamer's beat.
With popcorn clouds and soda stars,
Each nap's a film that's truly ours.

I laugh at plots of banana slips,
As characters take their silly trips.
But just as love stories bloom and sway,
The alarm clock jabs, and dreams decay.

Yet in this intermission, I recline,
With fantasies, I sip on sunshine.
A fleeting dance of whimsy and cheer,
Until reality gives a sneaky leer.

When curtains close on slumber's stage,
I fight to stay, but turn the page.
A matinee that begs a reprise,
For laughter lives where daytime lies.

Threads of Thoughts in Twilight

At twilight's edge, my mind does weave,
Threads of thoughts that twist and cleave.
Between the seams of snooze and wake,
   I ponder all my choices, make.

   Like tangled yarn of vibrant hue,
   Ideas float like clouds that brew.
   Words are bouncing, light as air,
     As I nap lightly in my chair.

Yet morning's call, a raspy tune,
Soon teases me beneath the moon.
But in this twilight, where dreams are spun,
   Each nap is a race I've somehow won.

   I cherish moments, fleeting, brief,
   In soft retreat from time's belief.
With giggles caught on evening's breeze,
   I find my joy between the Z's.

Chasing Shadows of Intent

I dream of sandwiches piled high,
While pillows beckon with a sigh.
Chasing crumbs of thought and snack,
In blissful doze, I lose the track.

The world outside just keeps on racing,
While I'm in here, a nap embracing.
Intentions blurred by snoozing time,
Only wake for salad, not for rhyme.

My plans lie snoozing next to me,
As seconds drip like honey tea.
I sketch a life of grand design,
But oh, how peaceful is this line!

So let the hours roll on by,
I'll search for purpose in the sky.
Between the blinks, a chuckle grows,
In joyful naps, my wisdom shows.

Quiet Conversations with Time

Time whispers soft upon my cheek,
As I drape 'neath this woolly peak.
Each tick and tock, a lullaby,
In dreams, I learn to soar and fly.

With cozy blankets, I'll confide,
In this stillness, where thoughts abide.
What to do with life so vast?
Oh well, one more nap—let's make it last!

Alone with thoughts that spin and dance,
I ponder if I missed my chance.
But laughter bubbles in my mind,
As sleep's embrace is sweetly kind.

So here I am, amidst the snores,
A half-awake philosopher in wars.
With every nap, a new insight,
That sometimes life is just delight.

The Riddle of the Restful

In cozy corners, questions swell,
What's the secret? Time will tell.
A riddle wrapped in dreams so bright,
Should I rise or just recite?

I ponder puns and silly quips,
While snuggled tight, I map my trips.
The journey starts beneath my sheets,
With trail mix dreams and snacky feats.

Questions float like clouds above,
Where inspiration meets a shove.
Is it wisdom found in snooze,
Or just another nap I choose?

A nap, a laugh, a slumber vault,
In rhythm, life begins to halt.
The riddle—solve it with a grin,
When waking up is where we win.

Epiphanies in the Drowsy Hours

When eyelids weigh like hefty trees,
Epiphanies dance on a gentle breeze.
The world's whirring fades away,
As drowsy thoughts begin to play.

In twinkling light of afternoon,
I ponder puzzles on a tune.
Ideas shimmer like starlit dreams,
Within the whispers of nap-time schemes.

Do I need to climb great heights?
Or can I find them in cozy nights?
In dozing depths, I find my way,
With chuckles soft that softly sway.

As laughter lingers in the air,
I chase my thoughts without a care.
In every snooze, a bright surprise—
The meaning hides in sleepy eyes.

Morning Thoughts Wrapped in Covers

Under blankets, dreams collide,
Coffee waits, my cozy guide.
Pillows speak of silly schemes,
Reality slips, or so it seems.

In snooze land, logic takes a ride,
Plans to conquer, all denied.
Whispers of the day ahead,
Are silenced by my sleepy head.

Each tick of time, a quick escape,
In this realm, I feel quite great.
The world can wait, I softly grin,
While wrestling drowsiness within.

Who needs goals when dreams are vast?
In warm embraces, I've an ideal cast.
A life on pause, and yet so grand,
As blankets cradle my lazy stand.

Tapestry of Time in Dreamspace

In dreamspace, hours weave a thread,
Naps turn moments into dread.
Time is friendly, it bends and flops,
As I swim in a sea of soft hops.

I chase the sun with slumber's braid,
Reality's grip is gently frayed.
The fabric filled with fanciful tales,
What a joy, my day derails!

A nap today, another tomorrow,
With pastel dreams chasing sorrow.
What's the rush? Oh, let it pass,
As I dream of life's silly mass.

In this quilted time of chuckles and cheer,
I lounge in worlds that disappear.
A tapestry of rest divine,
Who knew that joy wanted to recline?

Reverberations of Half-Closed Eyes

In the hush of a lazy day,
Half-closed eyes start to sway.
Thoughts hop like a curious flea,
Chasing daydreams, oh so free.

A reverberation of sweet delight,
Caffeine whispers in lazy light.
The clock strikes nap, it's music to mine,
A quick comedy served with divine.

Floating on clouds of fluffy cheer,
Every tick feels like a year.
I ponder life and pizza slices,
As naps become my best devices.

The art of rest becomes my quest,
With winks exchanged, I jest and jest.
In this sluggish, funny trance,
I blitz through dreams, a dreamy dance.

The Gift of a Wandering Mind

A wandering mind, a gift in disguise,
Moments drift in sleepy sighs.
Adventure calls from the comfort zone,
As I journey far while I'm alone.

Imagined lands of cake and cream,
Where nothing's silly and all's a dream.
I hop on clouds of marshmallow fluff,
In a realm where life is never rough.

Fields of laughter, naps come in waves,
Every joke, my psyche saves.
Thoughts collide like a wacky play,
As I lounge in bliss, come what may.

Snoozing softly, my mind's heart glows,
With every giggle, my spirit grows.
Between the dreams, the real me beams,
In this gift of naps, life's fun-filled themes.

Interludes of Existence

In the cozy nook where dreams collide,
The cat plots schemes, full of feline pride.
A yawn escapes as eyelids descend,
Who knew napping could be such a trend?

With snacks at hand and pillows all around,
Our greatest insights wait, simply unbound.
Postponing our thoughts for a quick little doze,
Reckless wisdom often just comes and goes.

Between one snooze and the next little snack,
Ideas bounce in a playful attack.
We wake with a grin, ready to engage,
Life's great mystery: a nap on the page!

So let the world ponder as we snooze on,
Finding adventure 'til the new dawn.
Half awake, with a chuckle and cheer,
Who knew finding joy could start with a leer?

Half-Shut Eyes

With eyes half-shut, the world drifts away,
Reality feels like a game we can play.
A brief little slumber can spark such delight,
As dreams offer laughter—a whimsical flight.

The clock spins wildly, but we don't care,
As visions of snacks float madly in air.
A sandwich, a donut, a whole parade feast,
Our nap-time reveries, to say the least!

We rise like legends, bold and inspired,
With fluffy ambitions that gently transpired.
"Did I solve world peace or invent a new snack?"
An honest inquiry; we'll never look back.

So nestle in close and surrender to dreams,
In the land of our snooze, nothing's as it seems.
Life, in its humor, reveals as it goes,
Finding joy in the simple, where the silliness flows!

Open Hearts

With open hearts, we embrace the unknown,
In the valley of pillows, where comfort is grown.
Dreams are our canvas, sleepy and bright,
We paint them with giggles, chuckles take flight.

With snacks like confetti scattered all around,
We gather our thoughts, they flourish unbound.
A whisper of wisdom between each sweet cheer,
Who knew life's interest lay snuggled near?

Our minds take a leap just as eyelids fall,
The world gets ridiculous, but we love it all.
Awakening slowly, with stories to tell,
Our laughter resounds, we're under its spell.

As dawn's gentle light taps at the door,
We cherish the moments, the laughter in store.
So nap if you must, and play if you dare,
Life's wackiest wonders are found in mid-air!

Between Shadows and Daylight

Between shadows cast and daylight so bright,
We drift on a ship made of dreams and delight.
A wink and a nod, then the humor unfolds,
In the land of the snooze, surprises are told.

The blankets are cloaks, the pillows—our throne,
In this kingdom of rest, we're never alone.
An army of snacks rallies round with a grin,
As gales of laughter dance softly within.

A nap is a ticket to places untold,
With each little slumber, new magic unfolds.
We rise from our dreams, with a snicker and cheer,
Who says wisdom's found? It's the snacks, it's the beer!

So linger a moment in the hush of the morn,
Where slumber and giggles gently are born.
With life's myst'ry wrapped in a cozy embrace,
In the wander of dreams, we find our own pace!

Snooze and Discover

To snooze is to ponder, to dream and explore,
In the realms of our cushions, new worlds we'll adore.
A giggle afoot, as eyelids grow heavy,
Our minds build empires where chaos is leveled.

With snacks on the table, we take a great dive,
Between bites and chuckles, we truly arrive.
The wisdom of napping, a treasure to keep,
With silly old musings that bloom from the sleep.

Each snooze opens portals to laughter so grand,
Where dreams merge like planets aligned in a band.
"Did I invent a car that runs on pure haste?"
Who knows where we land when our thoughts go to waste?

So settle in snug, let the adventures begin,
In the winking hours where dreams are our kin.
Life's sweetest moments arrive with a nod,
From the depths of our slumber, they spring forth like God!

The Serenade of Snooze

In the arms of a comfy chair,
Dreams unravel without a care.
Pillows sing a lullaby,
As I drift and gently sigh.

Sandman's got his midnight call,
Whispers weave, then softly fall.
Oh, the wisdom of a yawn,
Life's great truths, all but gone.

Sleepy thoughts begin to churn,
While the world outside does turn.
Jokes emerge from zzzz's sound,
In soft laughter, joy is found.

Between the blinks and cozy freeze,
Snippets of life come with ease.
Napping's art, a quirky dance,
Every snooze, a second chance.

Horizons in the Hazy

The sun dips low, my eyelids weigh,
See the world in a blurry sway.
In a daze, my thoughts take flight,
Chasing dreams in hazy light.

Time slips by in gentle bends,
Laughter echoes, giggles send.
Sleepy musings share their charm,
As my mind drifts like a farm.

At times I ponder, what's the cost?
Of moments gained, yet naps are lost.
But in each snooze, I clearly see,
Life's odd truths unraveling free.

In the mist of a midday break,
Funny insights start to wake.
Shadows dance, and smiles play,
In this wakeful nap ballet.

The Flicker of Insight in Drowsiness

A blink, a nod, the couch's embrace,
Sudden thoughts begin to race.
Wisdom sprouts from dreamlike haze,
In slumber's grip, I feel amazed.

Silly ideas in sleepy flow,
Like a movie with a flip of a toe.
Thoughts like marshmallows puff and bounce,
As the mind drifts and flops, it pounce!

In the depths of dozing strife,
Flashy thoughts, oh what a life!
Quirky dreams and chuckles meet,
In this cartoonish nap retreat.

Awake, I share my witty finds,
As laughter dances in our minds.
Half a snooze, and here we are,
Chasing dreams, our twinkling star.

Streams of Consciousness as We Nap

In a world where pillows reign,
Thoughts are wild, vision's insane.
As I drift, I make a plan,
For a kingdom of a napping fan.

Clouds of fluff and giggles swirl,
In the stillness, ideas unfurl.
Tickle my brain, let's have some fun,
As daydreams dance, the nap's begun.

Beneath the eyelids, life's a game,
Attributes change, it's never the same.
Funny tales from a sleepy start,
In my cozy little heart.

From the realm of snoozes grand,
Witty insights hand in hand.
Laugh and sigh, the world's our stage,
Napping, dreaming, at every age.

Suspenders of Time

When clocks tick slow and eyelids droop,
Dreams dive deep, like a fish in soup.
In the laughter of snores, we float and drift,
Cuddled in blankets, a whimsical gift.

Between z's and yawn, the world spins round,
A dance with shadows, where joy is found.
Tick, tock in chaos, it all feels so right,
As logic takes naps in the soft moonlight.

Time wears suspenders, so quirky and bold,
Holding the moments that can't be controlled.
Dragons of daytime, with wings made of light,
Fight off the sorrows that lurk in the night.

So let's toast to slumber, our jovial friend,
With each dozing second, the giggles ascend.
In a world made of pillows, where silliness reigns,
We'll dance on the clouds till the morning complaints.

Stories Told in the Silences

In between whispers, where snores intermingle,
Tales of the ridiculous begin to tingle.
Dreams wear costumes, like jesters on stage,
Spinning their yarns onto the next page.

The silence is loud, a raucous delight,
In the absence of sound, we take flight.
Feathers of thoughts float, collecting in heaps,
Painting the walls while the whole world sleeps.

Giggles erupt in the still of a nap,
Frogs in tuxedos lead the wild clap.
Tickles of laughter, caught in mid-air,
As stories unfold in the land of nowhere.

So let's pause for the moments, the sweet interludes,
Where silence speaks volumes and joy is infused.
Between the sleigh rides of dreams and of sighs,
The humor of life finds its way to the skies.

Chu's Rest

In the land of Chu, where the clouds do nest,
Naps are the rulers, granting us rest.
Every cat curls up with a grin oh so wide,
In a kingdom of cushions, we take a glide.

The sun winks softly, as dreams start to play,
Whispering secrets in a hilarious way.
Jellies of jellybeans float in the air,
While horses wear pajamas, without a care.

Who needs a clock when it's all a facade?
In Chu's realm of laughter, we give time a nod.
The bed is our court, where we rule as we please,
As the world spins like tops, and we giggle with ease.

So nestle in soft, let your worries drift,
In the land of Chu, take the jest as a gift.
For in every snooze, there's a story to glean,
Of sleepy adventures and moments unseen.

Mind's Play

Through curtains of dreams, the thoughts freely escape,
Twirling like dancers in a whimsical shape.
A jester in the mind throws a pie from afar,
As giggles of nonsense shine bright like a star.

In the land of the z's, where the oddities dwell,
Parrots wear capes and the owls cast a spell.
Tickled by visions that twist and that spin,
Each nap is a carnival, laughter cradled within.

Chasing the chuckles, we glide and we swoop,
Floating on marshmallows, a bouncy loop.
With every deep breath, hilarity teems,
As mischief unfurls in the fabric of dreams.

So let's frolic through slumber, in hilarity's clutch,
Delighting in giggles, oh it tickles so much.
In the playground of thought, where the silly ones play,
Naps draw out smiles in a wonderful way.

Mandalas of the Mind

In spirals of slumber, our thoughts intertwine,
Creating bold patterns in a dance so divine.
A wheel of imagination spins wild and free,
As nap-time artists paint the air with glee.

Round and round we go, in the twirl of a dream,
Twirling like ice skaters, life's funny theme.
With each gentle pulse, the cosmos chuckles,
As the sleepyheads venture into grand huddles.

Sketching our laughter on clouds made of fluff,
In the mandalas woven, it's never enough.
The hug of the sheets whispers secrets so sweet,
A rebellious reminder, laughter's a treat.

So join in the journey, take a snooze with delight,
A tapestry of joy is painted each night.
With every blink, we explore the absurd,
In the mandalas of dreams, where the laughter is heard.

Dreaming with Purpose

In the midst of a daytime snooze,
I ponder great thoughts, my mind does cruise.
To conquer the couch, my noble quest,
I stretch and yawn, for sleep's the best.

With snacks in hand, I bravely dream,
A warrior's fight, or so it seems.
As I drift off in fluffy delight,
My pillow whispers, 'Just hold on tight!'

The world outside spins, all a blur,
While I unravel each creative spur.
Nap time nobly marshals the arc,
As visions take flight when it's dark.

Awake with a snort, my mission unclear,
But laughter erupts, bringing good cheer.
These moments, I swear, bring pure fun,
In the realm of dreams, oh what a run!

Siesta Serenity

The clock ticks loudly, oh what a ploy,
It whispers sweetly, 'Take a nap, oh boy!'
With a cat on my lap, dreams softly blend,
I drift through the clouds, sweet naps never end.

A sandwich awaits, just out of reach,
But my eyelids drop, they start to teach.
In slumber I plot, schemes both wild and quaint,
While my faithful snack grows a little faint.

As sunbeams dance on my snoozing form,
I invent strange tales where laughter is born.
A landslide of giggles, todo so sly,
My nap at two-thirty, oh me, oh my!

Awake with a snore, it's humor divine,
I rise like a phoenix, far out of line.
For what's a great nap without a good laugh?
In the kingdom of snooze, I take my half!

Awakening to Clarity

I close my eyes for a moment, just so,
The world spins away, like fresh-fallen snow.
In my comfort zone, ideas appear,
Every snore brings a muse that feels near.

Suddenly, a thought? Or just the cat's tail?
I ponder great truths in the midst of a fail.
With each restful blink, clarity grows,
Mixing giggles and dreams in a raucous flow.

The richness of napping, a curious dance,
Each dream, it seems, grows a bit of chance.
As I contemplate snacks, like a sage,
I realize my glory lies in this stage.

With a stretch and a sigh, I rise from my throne,
A regal snoozer, by comfy winds blown.
This nap is no waste, it's filled with good lore,
A snapshot of joy I truly adore!

The Art of Waking Up

A battle each morning, oh what a sight,
To prod and to poke, where's my will to fight?
With blankets like mountains, I scheme and I plot,
To outsmart the urge of that cozy spot.

An alarm for my heart, it buzzes in vain,
As I roll to my side, experiencing pain.
The pillows conspire to keep me in dreams,
With plots so absurd, or so it seems.

Once up for the day, my thoughts run amok,
I search for my keys, feel a bit out of luck.
Yet amidst all the chaos, I chuckle and cheer,
For each twist of the morning brings laughter, my dear.

So here's to the naps and those goofy sleep fights,
To waking up laughing when sleep's caught in flight.
Each day isn't wild unless dreams take a spin,
So nap like a pro and let giggles begin!

www.ingramcontent.com/pod-product-compliance
Lightning Source LLC
Chambersburg PA
CBHW051648160426
43209CB00004B/838